Bootlegger's Bluff

Poems by K.W. Peery

Kansas City Spartan Press Missouri

Spartan Press
Kansas City, Missouri
spartanpresskc.com

Copyright (c) Kevin W. Peery, 2018
First Edition 1 3 5 7 9 10 8 6 4 2
ISBN: 978-1-946642-66-0
LCCN: 201853739

Design, edits and layout: Jason Ryberg
Cover and author photo: Kevin W. Peery
All rights reserved. No part of this publication may be reproduced or transmitted in any form or by any means, electronic or mechanical, including photocopying, recording or by info retrieval system, without prior written permission from the author.

Spartan Press would like to thank Prospero's Books, The Fellowship of N-finite Jest, The Prospero Institute of Disquieted P/o/e/t/i/c/s, Will Leathem, Tom Wayne, Jeanette Powers, j. d. tulloch, Jon Bidwell, Jason Preu, Mark McClane, Tony Hayden and the whole Osage Arts Community.

CONTENTS

Boogie in the Dark / 1

Trooper Cox / 3

Browning / 5

Psychedelic Sunset / 7

Magic Bullet / 9

Shell-Shocked Six / 11

Slow Sip with Skip / 12

Moonlight & Gin / 13

Route 66 Motel / 15

Thunder in the Wind / 16

Schaefer's Instead / 17

Devil's Elbow / 19

Bird's Foot / 21

Hell on a High Rail / 23

Half Spent Zin / 25

Deadbolt Donnie / 27

Last Gasp / 29

Square Shine Jugs / 31

Old Timer / 33

Phantom Train / 35

Harry's Storm / 37

Booze & Benzos / 38

Stash / 40

Smashed / 42

Silver Bullets & Shit-House Luck / 44

Gospel Lounge / 46

Rockland Trust / 48

Steve Cropper's Shitter / 50

Waco Weed / 52

Goddamn Alproazolam / 54

Razor Burn Sunrise / 55

Faster Than Before / 57

Sixteen Headshots / 59

Six Miles South of Sunflower / 61

This Web / 63

More Than Friends / 65

Olde E / 66

Shootin' the Bull / 67

Salt Shack / 69

Precipice / 70

Hungry for Better Blues / 71

Bettye Lavette / 73

Stranded / 75

Overpriced Oxblood Wingtips / 77

Moments Before the Storm / 79

This book is for Peeve.

Boogie in the Dark

We
were
almost
outta
ammo
and
on
the
wrong
side
of
the
Linn
County
line...

When
Richard
hit
the
headlights
and
dropped
the
hammer
in
his

Sixty-
Eight
Judge

While
a
drunk
Jimmy
Reed
played
Boogie
in
the
Dark

Trooper Cox

We
were
three
miles
South
of
Trenton
when
Trooper
Cox
pulled
us
over…

And
it
was
the
last
goddamn
time
we
would
ever
haul
shine
or

pay
a
fine
across
the
line
in
Grundy
County

Browning

The
last
time
we
had
balls
big
enough
to
roll
through
Browning
after
Midnight…
we'd
been
drinkin'
Budweiser
bottles
in
the
backseat
of
Brenda's
burnished
brown
Buick
Skylark…

Chain
smokin'
a
stolen
pack
of
Salem
100's…
while
listenin'
to
Ric
Ocasek
sing
the
blues

Psychedelic Sunset

We were
cruisin'
the duals
out on
Deer Creek
road...
in my
cousin's
Sixty-Seven
Eldorado...

Smokin' loaded
Swisher Sweets
and
listenin' to
Bootsy Collins
sing
*I'd Rather
Be With You...*

When
the left
rear tire
blew...
and
everything
we

thought
we
knew...
vanished
like
the
psychedelic
sunset
always
said
she
would

Magic Bullet

There's a
magic bullet
in this
limestone
glass...
that was
triple distilled...
just to
save my
ass...

Been here
in the
shade
since the
church bells
rang...
got the
Sunday blues...
in this
old porch
swing...

There's a
magic bullet...
here on
Mark Twain lane...

gotta
Huckleberry high
and a
Pudd'nhead
brain...

Just listenin'
to Elvis...
sing
Kentucky
Rain...
while
I bite
the bullet
and curse
these
veins

Shell-Shocked Six

I'm
just
sittin'
here...
sippin'
cold
beer...
holdin'
this
shell-
shocked
six
of
Clubs...

Wonderin'
if
bluffin'
them
again...
will
somehow
be
enough...
to
save
me
from
myself

Slow Sip with Skip

With
my
autopilot
engaged
on
this
dark
shadow
haze…
I'll
slow
sip
some
sherry
wood
single
malt
and
listen
to
Skip
James
sing
the
Cypress
Grove
Blues

Moonlight & Gin

Traces of
moonlight
through
a bottle
of gin….
this
Hendrick's
buck
is bound
to win…

A race
against
time…
urgencies
bitch…
traces of
moonlight
where
most men
quit…

Traces of
moonlight
at 2AM…
a contorted
view

and
crooked
grin…

Just three
more lines...
till the
walls
cave in...
and traces
of moonlight
through
a bottle
of gin

Route 66 Motel

Two days
after hittin'
the California Coast
Credit Union
in Temecula…
we were
holed up
at the
Route 66 Motel…
with a case
of Evan Williams
and four
Black Bear burgers…

It was a
perfect plan…
to let the heat
die down…
while we
waited to
make our
next move
in Escondido

Thunder in the Wind

There's a
small part of me
in Joshua Tree…
still searchin' for
the strength
to sing
the *Brass Button*
blues…

Where
her words
burn eternal
in the warm
evening Sun
and Gram's voice
still echoes
like thunder
in the wind

Schaefer's Instead

We were
seven miles
East
of Quincy
Illinois
when
the pills
kicked
in...

And
if I
knew
then...
what was
waitin'
for us
at
Regions
Bank
in
Decatur...

We woulda
rolled
on South
to

Saint
Peter
and
spent
the
afternoon
at
Schaefer's
instead

Devil's Elbow

On
the outskirts
of Devil's
Elbow...
we saw a
one armed
man
with a
three legged
dog...
sellin'
hand painted
snappin' turtle
shells
outta the
trunk
of his
75 Impala...

He was
wearin'
a wide
brimmed
straw hat...
chain smokin'
Kool 100s...
n'
singin'

Ain't No Sunshine...
in
the
afternoon
rain

Bird's Foot

This
crooked trail
I'm on
is cloaked
in pink lilac
and lavender…

It's a
Bird's Foot
oasis…
where
I go
to escape
the internal
noise…

A
last ditch
effort to
soak up
the
silence…

Where
my tears
taste like
Tres Agaves…

And
ancient sins
can be
laid to
rest

Hell on a High Rail

When
I
heard
her
muffled
screams...
bleedin'
through
the
blistered
blue
door
of
room
two
sixteen...

I
racked
the
slide
on
my
.45...
and
sent
her

kidnapper
to
Hell
on
a
high
rail

Half Spent Zin

There
was
a
half
spent
bottle
of
Bedrock
Zinfandel
standin'
at
attention
on
his
mahogany
dining
room
table...

And
if
we
only
knew...
his
twisted
version

of
the
truth...
we
might
have
let
him
live
just
long
enough
to
kill
it

Deadbolt Donnie

Deadbolt Donnie
drove a
72 Ford
Ranchero
in grabber
blue...

It was
really
the only
thing
he had
left
in the
end...

And despite
our best
efforts
to help
him...
Donnie
died
the way
he always
said
he would...

Ridin'
in style...
at the
bottom
of
Lake
Killarney

Last Gasp

Carlos
said
shootin'
those
sneaky
bastards
wasn't
nearly
as
hard
as
he
thought
it
would
be...

But
at
over
seventeen
hundred
yards
away...
that
last
gasp

through
the
glass
always
looks
the
same

Square Shine Jugs

Dean
would come
down
from Detroit
every September
to pick up
a batch
of our
best…

So
we'd stuff
the trunk
of his
Buick Riviera
with more
square
shine jugs
than you've
ever seen…

And while
he drank
his weight
in whiskey…
we would
take the

rest of
his travel
cash…
one
crooked
hand
at a
time

Old Timer

There's
an edge
on this
Old Timer
that's always
thirsty for
more...
and
no matter
how many
I skin...
the blade
stays
sharp...

Sometimes
I use it
when I
need a
close shave...
then nick
myself
on purpose
just to
watch the

pink water
swirl
in our
bone white
bathroom
sink

Phantom Train

The
Phantom Train
travels along
an abandoned
loop line
out in
Eastern
Kentucky...

It's
chock-full
of sinners' souls...
in route
to their next
destination...

The
Phantom Train
rolls slow
across the
Cumberland
plateau...
where
black lungs
cough
coal dust
into a

bottomless
chasm...

There's
a one-eyed
conductor
with a
shit eatin'
grin
and a
well stocked
bar car
with the
doors
welded
shut

Harry's Storm

There was
no hate
left in
Harry's heart...
as thunder
shook the
lightnin' rod
sideways
on that
ole crib barn
off Calico Road
in rural
Linn County...

And as
he held
the loaded
Ruger
against his
silver painted
temple...
the only
storm
still ragin'
was the one
he had left
outside

Booze & Benzos

The
booze
and benzos
never really
made things
better...
but they
sure as hell
fueled
my madness
and internal
sadness
in ways
I'd never
dreamt
before...

It was like
sleepwalkin'
on two
swollen feet...
across
the moonlit
glow
of a
rosewood
floor...

Just
moments
before
I would
press this
cold snubnose
against my
silver painted
temple
and
wait
patiently
while
all the
nerve
bled
out

Stash

I
used
to
wrap
my
better
prescription
pills
in
a
brand
new
Gold
Toe
sock...

Then
secure
them
in
a
cinched
Crown
Royal
bag...
before
stashin'

that
plush
purple
pouch
in
the
spare
tire
space
of
my
88
Sedan
DeVille

Smashed

For five
fast years
I tried
hard
to convince
myself
that pills
were
pre-scored
for the
ease
of my
sublingual
satisfaction...

A
thirty
milligram
chain
reaction...

Where
sweet orange
rounds...
were crashin'
upside down...

Just
smashed
there
to snort...
every
half-life
short

And
no magic
on the
mirror
could
save
me

Silver Bullets & Shit-House Luck

I
was
stoned
and
all
alone
the
night
death
came
callin'...
N'
if
it
weren't
for
silver
bullets
and
shit-
house
luck...
my
ass
woulda

been
grass
long
before
Mickey
ever
mentioned
Memphis

Gospel Lounge

I
was
just
sittin'
here
alone
in
the
Gospel
Lounge
at
Knuckleheads
Saloon...
when
my
guardian
angel
appeared...

She
tried
to
resign...
citing
my

sudden
decline...
and
wouldn't
even
buy
me
a
beer

Rockland Trust

I
was
wearin'
a
walnut
Stetson
Stratoliner
and
brand
new
pinstripe
suit...
on
the
afternoon
we
hit
Rockland
Trust
in
Hyannis
Port...

It
was
an
easy

score
there
along
the
shore...
where
no
one
could
dream
we
would
do
it

Steve Cropper's Shitter

My friend
Bryant
called from
Nashville
this mornin'
to tell me
his boss
sent him
to work on
a clogged shitter
at Steve Cropper's
house…

And all
I could think
to say was —

Man…
you can't leave
without askin'
ole Steve
about the time
in Sixty-Nine…
when Otis
needed

his help
to finish
(Sittin' On) The Dock of the Bay
just three days
before his
charter plane
crashed into
Lake Monona

Waco Weed

We
ran weed
outta Waco
for about
ten months
back in
07...

Just
to pay
for the
cocktail
of prescriptions...
Juanita
needed
to treat
her
pancreatic
cancer...

And while
dealin' drugs
wasn't our
usual means
of survival...

This
last-gasp
gamble
was all
we could
afford
at the
time

Goddamn Alproazolam

This goddamn
Alprazolam
has fried
my insides
to the point
that I
can't even
remember
what it
feels like
to sink my
calloused toes
in the
Springtime cold
of this
riverbed
sand

Razor Burn Sunrise

It
was
a
razor
burn
sunrise
last
Sunday...

The
kind
that
keeps
Ray-
Ban
in
business...

And
I
know
it
may
seem
strange...

But
I'd
rather
watch
it
rain...
than
ride
to
church
with
the
windows
down

Faster Than Before

Gin
drunk
on
a
high
wire...
staring
at
death's
reflection
in
a
fractured
hand
mirror...

Foolish
and
fading...
fearing
that
this
round
could
be
my
last...

Hoping
the
fall
to
the
valley
floor
is
a
little
faster
than
before

Sixteen Headshots

They
all
claim
Chuck's
aim
was
as
steady
as
a
surgeon's
scalpel…

His
accuracy
at
times
unparalleled…

Like
on
Valentine's
Day
of
69…
when
Chuck

used
his
M40
to
make
sixteen
headshots
in
the
afternoon
rain

Six Miles South of Sunflower

When the
Mississippi
State Patrol
stopped us
six miles
South
of Sunflower...

We were
haulin'
weapons
outta the
Big Easy...
to trade
for prescription
pills in
Chapel Hill
Tennessee...

And when
Wayne
told the
trooper
we were
on our way
to a
funeral
in Huntsville...

He cut
our asses
loose...
without
even runnin'
our fake
ID's

This Web

Within
this
web...
are
the
words
I
weave...
Like
bullets
before
the
flop...
with
one
up
my
sleeve...
Just
a
bootlegger's
bluff...
when
I'm
in
too
deep...

Within
this
web...
writin'
words
I
need....
Yeah...
within
this
web...
where
you'll
find
me

More Than Friends

Her
fingers
trace
this
whiskey
glass...
like
she
knows
where
I've
been...
And
I'm
still
not
sure...
what
to
say
to
her...
that'll
make
us
more
than
friends

Olde E

Forty ounces
of charcoal filtered
liquid amnesia
will only
set ya back
two fifty two
at Traino's

And that's
a small
price to pay
at two
in the mornin'…
when pissin'
my pants
at Waffle House
will seem
like the
best damn
business
decision
I've made
all day

Shootin' the Bull

We would
both buy
a six of
Schlitz
Malt
Liquor
at Ace
Package
after
school…
then
roll down
to
Grand
River
and find
an old
log
to set
our
empties
on

I
always
packed

a thirty

eight

special…

so

we'd

take

turns

Shootin' the Bull

till all

twelve

Tall Boy's

took

a spill

into

the

damn

dirty

drink

Salt Shack

The smell
of a
slaughterhouse
salt shack
in mid-July...
can make
a grown man
cry...

When he
sees
the size
of those
maggots...
feedin'
on bloody
beef hides...
stacked up
like a
deck of
Doyle's room
playin' cards
just waitin'
to be
shuffled
again

Precipice

Here
alone
at
the
edge
of
the
precipice...

With
a
gutful
of
guilt...
in
blind
desperation...

Knowin'
full
well...
I
should've
recognized
this
Hell
years
ago

Hungry for Better Blues

We were
shootin'
turtle doves
off the
overhead
power lines
with my
brother's
Browning
A-5...
on the
same
afternoon
lung cancer
killed
Clarence
Gatemouth
Brown...

And even
now...
when
I begin
to spin
Sometimes I Slip...

it makes
me sad
about that
September...
and hungry
for better
blues

Bettye Lavette

I love
listenin' to
Bettye LaVette
skin a
Dylan
song...

Ya know...
there's
more
goddamn
soul
in one
of her
pinkie toes
than
ole Bob
could
possibly
grasp...

And she's still
kickin' ass
on stage
at 72...
with
a signature

rasp
that bleeds
pure blues...

Yeah... I
love listenin' to
Bettye LaVette
skin a
Dylan
song...
and I'll
betcha
ole Bob
does
too

Stranded

Stranded here
at the
Hampton Inn
off Cicero
Avenue...
I'm
down to
the last
greasy slice
of Giordano's
deep dish...
with one
more
40 ounce
sink beer
to wash
it all
down...
I've already
drunk dialed
the front
desk...
for a
6AM
wake-up
call...

And
if this
lake effect
snow
lifts
in time...
I'll
be back
in Kansas City
before Joe's
opens
at eleven

Overpriced Oxblood Wingtips

On that
warm
Saturday
afternoon
in June...
my brand new
Brooks Brothers
shoes...
were as
shiny
as the
ocean blue
marble tiles
in Bridget's
Malibu
beach house...
And
if we
weren't
forced
to be
there
for a
funeral
dinner
that day...

I might
remember
more...
than
the sheen
on her
floor...
or my
overpriced
oxblood
wingtips

Moments Before the Storm

Beneath
moonlit
shattered
branches...
we
made
our
way
past
unmarked
graves
and
buried
the
only
remaining
evidence
linking
us
to
the
crime...

And
over
time...

we
would
almost
forget...
how
calm
the
oak
leaves
were...
just
moments
before
the
storm
rolled
in

Americana songwriter and Kansas-City-based storyteller K.W. Peery is the author of five poetry collections: *Tales of a Receding Hairline; Purgatory; Wicked Rhythm; Ozark Howler; Gallatin Gallows*. *Tales of a Receding Hairline* was a semifinalist in the Goodreads Choice Awards – Best in Poetry 2016. Peery is a regular contributor in *Veterans Voices Magazine*. His work is included in the Vincent Van Gogh Anthology *Resurrection of a Sunflower* and the Walsall Poetry Society Anthology, *Diverse Verse II & III*.

This project was made possible, in part, by generous support from the Osage Arts Community.

Osage Arts Community provides temporary time, space and support for the creation of new artistic works in a retreat format, serving creative people of all kinds — visual artists, composers, poets, fiction and nonfiction writers. Located on a 152-acre farm in an isolated rural mountainside setting in Central Missouri and bordered by ¾ of a mile of the Gasconade River, OAC provides residencies to those working alone, as well as welcoming collaborative teams, offering living space and workspace in a country environment to emerging and mid-career artists. For more information, visit us at www.osageac.org

Osage Arts Community

www.ingramcontent.com/pod-product-compliance
Lightning Source LLC
Chambersburg PA
CBHW020126130526
44591CB00032B/552

www.ingramcontent.com/pod-product-compliance
Lightning Source LLC
Chambersburg PA
CBHW020126130526
44591CB00032B/552